Survival Guides You Didn't Know You Needed

SURVIVING IN THE JUNGLE

Thomas Kingsley Troupe

BLACK RABBIT BOOKS

Hi Jinx is published by Black Rabbit Books
P.O. Box 3263, Mankato, Minnesota, 56002.
www.blackrabbitbooks.com
Copyright © 2018 Black Rabbit Books

Marysa Storm, editor; Michael Sellner, designer;
Catherine Cates, production designer;
Omay Ayres, photo researcher

Library of Congress Cataloging-in-Publication Data
Names: Troupe, Thomas Kingsley, author.
Title: Surviving in the jungle / by Thomas Kingsley Troupe.
Description: Mankato, Minnesota : Black Rabbit Books, [2018] |
Series: Hi jinx. Survival guides you didn't know you needed | Includes
bibliographical references and index.
Identifiers: LCCN 2017007265 (print) | LCCN 2017024685 (ebook)| ISBN
9781680723700 (e-book) | ISBN 9781680723403 (library binding)
Subjects: LCSH: Jungles–Juvenile humor. | Survival–Juvenile humor.
Classification: LCC PN6231.J86 (ebook) | LCC PN6231.J86 T76 2018 (print) | DDC
818/.602-dc23
LC record available at https://lccn.loc.gov/2017007265

Printed in China. 9/17

Image Credits

Alamy: Reuters, 20 (Ghinsberg); Dreamstime: Hanaschwarz, 11 (r bird);
Sunlight789, 11 (elephant); iStock: AnjaRabenstein, Cover (bkgd); hanaschwarz,
11 (l bird); Tigatelu, Cover (snake), 4 (snake); Shutterstock: Aji Pebriana, 1
(ostrich); Aliaksei_Z, 4 (two apes); Aluna1, 10–11 (bkgd); Andrey Makurin, 3
(bkgd); Angeliki Vel, 18 (sun); Arcady, 3 (note), 19 (note); BlueRingMedia,
8 (snake), 11 (kid); brux, 8 (bamboo), 20 (frog); Claudia Pylinskaya, 16–17
(boulders); dedMazay, 12 (worms); DM7, 2–3 (leg); Dreamcreation, Cover
(gorilla), 6 (frog), 15 (btm r fly); Dualororua, 1 (sloth); Ekler, 10 (torn
paper); frescomovie, Back Cover (bkgd); 15 (page bkgd); Galitsyn, 12
(parrot); GraphicsRF, Cover (bird), 4 (bkgd, mole, croc), 6–7 (jungle
bkgd), 15 (r squirrel), 16– 17 (lemurs); Gabrielle Erwart, 21 (footprints);
Ilya Chalyuk, 5, 9 (marker stroke), 13 (marker stroke), 16 (marker
stroke), 20 (marker stroke); Jeff Morin, 13 (worm); Ikeskinen, 7 (tiger);
Machinegunner, 7 (spider); Memo Angeles, Cover (kid), 4 (kid),
6–7 (puddle, rain), 8 (monkey), 14 (torn paper), 15 (kid, monkey,
leaves), 18 (boy); musicalryo, 12 (monkey); OkPic, 16–17 (stones);
opicobello, 6 (torn paper), 14; Pasko Maksim, Back Cover (top);
9 (torn paper), 17 (torn paper), 23 (torn paper); PePl, 15 (l fly);
pitju, 21 (curled edge); Pushkin, 15 (l squirrel); Ridjam, 15 (l
beetle); ridjam, 15 (blue bug); Rohit Dhanaji Shinde, 1 (elephant),
21 (elephant); Sarawut Padungkwan, 7 (boy); Studio Barcelona,
6 (leaf); Teguh Mujiono, 1 (tucan), 4 (r croc), 6 (frog, mosquito),
23; totallypic, 20 (arrow), zooco, 11 (deer); warawiri, 12 (monkey)
Every effort has been made to contact copyright holders for
material reproduced in this book. Any omissions will be rectified in
subsequent printings if notice is given to the publisher.

CONTENTS

Dear Reader,

To be honest, the author's **manuscript** wasn't supposed to become a book. There was a horrible mix up. You can keep reading, if you want. Just don't take any of these suggestions seriously.

Sincerely,
a very sorry editor

Chapter 1
AN ADVENTURE GONE WRONG

Clusters of insects chirp. Colorful birds sing from a tree not far away. A small stream bubbles in the distance. Leafy trees and thick **brush** grow all around you.

Being in a jungle doesn't sound too bad, right? But what if you're *lost* in the jungle? It could happen, you know! The jungle can be a deadly place if you're all alone.*

*Editor's Note: This was supposed to be a book about tigers! What was the author thinking?!

Time to Survive!

Animals approach! They lick their fangs, hungry for lost-person meat. Storms dump gallons of rain down on you. There's **quicksand** and poisonous bugs at every turn. The jungle is no joke!

Thankfully, you're prepared. You've got a survival guide you never thought you'd need. It's time to survive being alone in the jungle!

Famous Jungles
Amazon (in South America)
Congo (in Central Africa)
Corcovado (in Costa Rica)
Nainital (in India)

*Editor's Note: Tarzan isn't real. This idea is crazy.

Chapter 2
MEET YOUR NEW BEST FRIENDS

Being alone in the jungle can be, well, lonely. Since there aren't any people around, make friends with the animals. After all, it worked for Tarzan!*

The key to making animal pals is simple. Just learn their languages! Scratch your armpits and brush up on your monkey. Learn to hiss with the snakes. Chirp it up with the birds.

Parrots aren't the only birds that can "talk." Crows and ravens can too.

Befriend an Elephant

Not all animals are friendly, even if you can talk to them. So why not make nice with one of the big guys? Go ahead! Make an elephant your new best friend.

You'll feel like **royalty** riding an elephant. Plus, an elephant can knock mean animals out of the way. Prepare to **cruise** the jungle in style!

Elephants really do have good memories. So try not to do something embarrassing.

Chapter 3
TIME FOR
DINNER

To truly survive, you need to find food. Starving to death equals a zero percent chance at survival. But be careful. It is never smart to eat strange fruits. They can be poisonous!*

Instead, ask some animals what's good to eat. A monkey might have a banana malt recipe. Birds could help you spice up a worm sandwich. Just ask around!

About 90 percent of white, yellow, or green wild berries are poisonous. Only about 50 percent of red wild berries are safe to eat.

*Editor's Note: Wow! The author actually makes a good point about not eating strange fruit.

13

Salad

Sometimes animals don't like to share recipes. If so, make a green meal of your own. The jungle is your salad bar! Search for some leaves and vines. Tear the greens up, and enjoy a salad!*

It's important to make sure you get a healthy meal. Real survivors know having energy is necessary to escape alive. (Because you can't escape dead!)

Survival List
Use Food to Win Over Animal Friends

worms
(Birds like to eat early.)

fruits
(Monkeys will go ape over them.)

live mice
(Snakes love 'em!)

peanuts
(Elephants will always remember you for that.)

*Editor's Note: Some leaves can be poisonous too, so just skip the salad. Of course, someone smart wouldn't suggest something so dangerous.

15

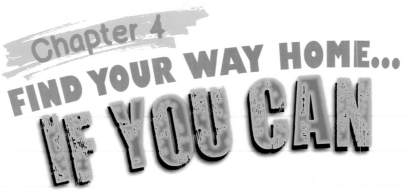

FIND YOUR WAY HOME...
IF YOU CAN

Let's face it. You don't want to live in the jungle forever. So put your brain to work! Try building a radio from wood and coconuts. Build a radio tower while you're at it.

Survival List
Ways to Signal for Help

visual signals
spell "HELP" or "SOS"

mirrors
use to reflect light

signal fires
Please don't burn the jungle to the ground.

There's an 89.2 percent chance the radio won't work.* So why not just make a sign? Find a clearing. Then collect rocks and branches. Use them to spell out "HELP, PLEASE" in big letters. People in an airplane will see your good manners. They will take you home.

*Editor's Note: No, there's a 100 percent chance the radio won't work. You can't make a radio from fruit.

Head North

Rescuers will sometimes take their time finding you. If you're tired of waiting, head north! In time, you'll leave the jungle. Keep walking until you find people, a phone booth, or a jetpack.

You never know when you'll be lost and alone in a jungle. It's noisy, full of bugs, and the food is pretty awful. But with this trusty guide, there's hope. You'll have a fighting chance of surviving!

The Amazon jungle is the world's largest rain forest. It covers more than 1.4 billion acres (595,697,265 hectares). So get walking!

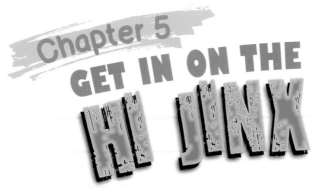

Chapter 5

GET IN ON THE HI JINX

It's fun to joke about getting lost, but it does happen in real life. In 1981, Yossi Ghinsberg explored the Amazon jungle with three other men. But his group soon broke up. Lost and alone, Ghinsberg wandered the jungle. He nearly drowned in a flood. He even fought off a jaguar. After three weeks, a search party found him.

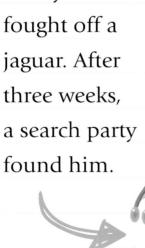

Take It One Step More

1. Getting lost anywhere can be scary. Think of a time when you were lost somewhere. What sort of tips helped you find your way?

2. There are all kinds of animals and bugs in the jungle. Do some research to discover the most dangerous jungle creatures.

3. What do you think the author of this book was thinking? If his suggestions are crazy, why did he write the book?

GLOSSARY

brush (BRUHSH)—short trees or shrubs

cruise (KROOZ)—to move along at a steady speed

manuscript (MAN-yuh-skript)—the original copy of a book before it has been printed

SOS—a signal used by ships and airplanes to call for help

quicksand (KWIK-sand)—deep, wet sand into which heavy objects sink easily

royalty (ROI-uhl-tee)—members of a royal family

BOOKS

Jackson, Tom. *The Amazon.* DK Eyewitness Books. New York: DK Publishing, 2015.

Rake, Matthew. *Creatures of the Rain Forest.* Real-Life Monsters. Minneapolis: Lerner Publications, 2016.

Wilkins, Mary-Jane. *Rain Forests.* Who Lives Here? Tucson, AZ: Brown Bear Books, 2017.

WEBSITES

10 Amazing Amazon Facts!
www.ngkids.co.uk/places/amazon-facts

Biomes: Tropical Rainforest
www.ducksters.com/science/ecosystems/rainforest_biome.php

Jungle Facts for Kids
www.scienceforkidsclub.com/jungles.html

INDEX